Park
Animals

A ZEBRA BOOK

Written by Wendy Boase
Illustrated by Barbara Firth

PUBLISHED BY
WALKER BOOKS
LONDON

Here is a frog
diving deep
as the rain falls.

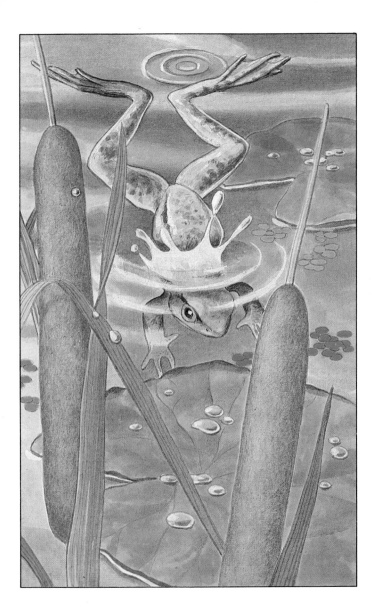

Here is a duck
paddling quickly
in the rain.

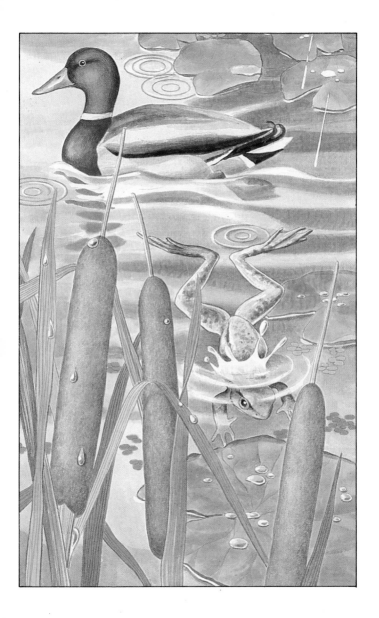

Here is a spider
running up
a wet branch.

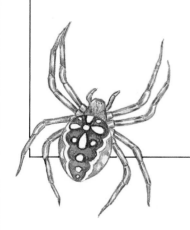

Here is a caterpillar
keeping dry under a leaf.

Here is a goldfinch
hopping into
her dry nest.

Here is a squirrel
darting up a tree
out of the rain.

The rain stops.
All the children come
to see the animals.

The goldfinch flaps her
wings and flies away.

The squirrel plays
with her babies.

The spider begins
to spin her web.

The duck waddles
on to the path.

The caterpillar wriggles
along the leaf.

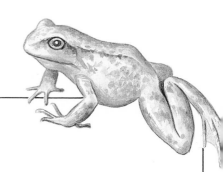

The frog sits
on a lily pad
in the sunshine.

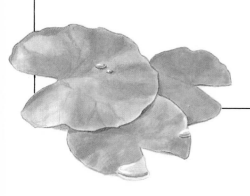